Journey To The Top

How To Reach Your Peak Performance Life

By Jamie Crosbie

Journey To The Top
How To Reach Your Peak Performance Life

Copyright © 2019 by ProActivate

All rights reserved. No part of this book may be reproduced or transmitted in any form or by any means without written permission from the author.

ISBN: 978-1704-103-044

~To my Mom, who was the greatest impact on helping me become who I was truly created to be. She lit up every room she entered and left everyone she touched better than before. She taught me to live life to the fullest and to live on purpose with purpose. I learned to celebrate life with zest and passion from my Mom. Campbell and Caden are lucky you left me with an incredible legacy that has made me the Mom I am today.

With gratitude and love,

Your Daughter~

Table of Contents:

Foreword by Alice R. Heiman............... 5

Foreword by Gerhard Gschwandtner 10

Chapter 1: *The Ascent Begins*................14

Chapter 2: *Live On Purpose With A Purpose*...24

Chapter 3: *Nothing To Fear*..................39

Chapter 4: *Optimism Always Wins*..........57

Chapter 5: *Tap Into Your Inner CEO*......69

Chapter 6: *Breaking The Ties That Bind You*..81

Chapter 7: *Release Limitations And Climb Higher*..94

Chapter 8: *Live In The Now*.................100

Chapter 9: *Purpose Beyond The Peak*...111

Foreword

"She believed she could, so she did."
R.S. Grey

When I was a little girl, my mother always told me that I could be anything I wanted and I believed her. I still do. Unfortunately, in elementary school there wasn't anyone to reinforce that with encouragement and worse there was discouragement. In the 60's they separated us by our IQ and put us in tracks to learn together.

Today, they don't put kids in tracks but a few minutes of observation in any school will clearly show who the teacher thinks are the smart ones.

Like me, you may have received mixed messages when you were young and those are part of what makes up your current mindset. As adults we may be held back by what we believe to be true about our ability and that dictates our mindset.

According to Merriam-Webster mindset is a mental attitude or inclination. A fixed state of mind. The first known use of the word was in the early 1900's and the study of mindset has been continuous.

Why now has it come to the forefront? Why so much talk about it, so many books on the topic, so many posts on social media?

In October of 2019, at the time I wrote this, I googled mindset and 150,000,000 results came up.

I believe that we are becoming more self-aware and as we look around and see those more successful, we wonder why.

Carol Dweck PhD, Yale graduate and professor of psychology at Stanford in my opinion is the mother of modern work on mindset. In fact, she wrote the pre-eminent book on it, Mindset: The New Psychology of Success in 2006.

Her book is the basis for all of us who continue to study and teach about mindset. Her work is considered ground-breaking.

Dweck's research has led her to conclude that there are two mindsets, the "fixed" mindset and the "growth" mindset.

A "fixed" mindset as defined by Dweck is one where you believe your success is based on innate ability. You either can or you can't. You are either smart enough or you're not.

A "growth" mindset as defined by Dweck is one where you believe your success is based on hard work, learning, training, and doggedness. If you don't know how to do something, you will figure it out or find someone who does to help you.

Although individuals may not be aware of their mindset, Dweck believes that you can figure out someone's mindset based on their behavior. This is very evident when it comes to reaction to failure. A person with a "fixed" mindset fears failure because they feel it reflects on their abilities. A person with a "growth" mindset approaches failure with the attitude that they can learn from it and improve.

Can one change their own mindset? People like Jamie and I agree, you can change your mindset.

Through her own challenges and struggles, belief and learning, Jamie has come to know that you can show others how to move from a fixed mindset to a growth mindset, changing their momentum and impacting their life for good.

Jamie developed a program to show others how to move from a fixed mindset to a growth mindset. In this book she reveals her process, sharing stories to illustrate and actions you can take immediately.

What is your mindset – fixed or growth? Maybe you are somewhere in between. If you are ready for a growth mindset, turn the page.

Alice R. Heiman

Growth Mindset, Life-long Learner, Believer in People

Founder of Alice Heiman, LLC and Co-Founder of TradeShow Makeover

P.S. Someone who loves Jamie very much.

Foreword

by Gerhard Gschwandtner
The Peak Performance Mindset

When Jamie Crosbie came to our Peak Performance Mindset training, I was so impressed with her passion for helping people improve their Mindset. A few months later, she stood on stage in front of a group of over 1,000 people; sharing her insights and tools for creating a Peak Performance Mindset. The thunderous applause was a great testimony of Jamie's talent as a speaker and her wisdom as a great teacher.

She took the concepts to the next level by opening up and sharing her own emotional roller coaster ride from the bliss of a perfect family, to deep disappointment and the dissolution of her marriage. On her healing journey she discovered her true, authentic self and transformed into a shining star. Jamie's story is living proof that a setback is nothing but a setup for a comeback. All that's needed is a Mindset shift.

The best way to explore your own mindset is to think of a Pyramid. At the bottom is the implanted Mindset. It contains all the experiences you had as a child. That includes what you learned from your parents or caretakers. That also includes all the negative experiences you had to endure as a child. These memories are often inaccurate or incomplete since they were created by a brain that hasn't been fully formed. View the implanted Mindset as a garden that has flowers and weeds. Your job as an adult is to water the flowers and stop watering the weeds.

At the second level of the pyramid is the imprinted Mindset. This level contains what you learned from your teachers, mentors, coaches and friends. Jim Rohn once said that you are the average of the five people you spend the most time with. If you want to achieve a level of success that's above average, you want to learn from people with a Mindset that's way above average. Surround yourself with people that lift you up and let go of people that hold you back.

The top level of the pyramid is the inspired Mindset. Everyone has it, but only few pay close attention to it. Remember the feeling you had the last time you reached the top of a mountain after a long hike? Or the feeling you get watching a beautiful sunset? You felt the gratitude and joy that comes from being in synch with nature. As you reflect on nature, you are conscious of your own unique nature and you realize that the magic you see on the outside also resides in you. You have inner magic. Everyone does. Mary Kay once said, "Most people die with their music still unplayed. They never dare to try." Jamie's book is a wake-up call for you to unleash your inner magic.

The Mindset tools that Jamie shares in this book can help you become more aware of your potential, more aware of your inner power, and more focused on your capabilities instead of your imagined shortcomings. Remember Jamie's message that everything you need to succeed is within you now. Cherish her book as your guide to discover and create the best version of you.

Chapter 1:
The Ascent Begins

This journey begins with a walk through an uncharted wilderness. Looking up and beyond a canopy of pine needles, a solitary mountain dominates the morning sky. At the end of this unbeaten, wooded path, a vast open field peppered with yellow and orange wildflowers surrounding the base of the mountain is revealed. This is the moment we've been waiting for.

This journey is more than a leisurely holiday appreciating nature. This is an odyssey for a true adventurer. This is a pilgrimage that many have dreamed of taking, but only a chosen few have dared to embark upon. Those that make it here, to the base of this mountain of dreams, arrive with the one aspiration of staking claim to the glory that awaits at the top. Every individual arriving at the mountain base comes from different walks of life. Whether they've climbed the summits of the Alps or walked up an extra flight of stairs at the office, everyone who makes it to this particular mountain shares one thing in common. They all have arrived to climb upward towards their purpose and claim their reward once they've reached the top.

This mountain represents the mental expedition taken by every brave individual in pursuit of success. Reaching the top of that mountain is undoubtedly an achievement. However, it is the journey from the base to the summit that offers the true reward of instilling a limitless mindset in each person that chooses to make this ascent.

Think about it. Similar to climbing that mountain, mentally ascending towards goals is a vertical movement; not a lateral shift. As it demands, this movement upward defies gravity. To a species accustomed to moving horizontally across solid ground, the mere notion of traveling any direction outside of that familiar line can be unfathomable to many. However, just because a concept is incomprehensible doesn't mean it's impossible.

So, what obstacle prevents more people from climbing upward towards a mountainous challenge? Is it the uncertainty of the unknown or lack of ambition that makes people cringe at the idea of rising to the occasion? Both are rooted within the same mental obstacle. Fear. The number one source of fear is us. We are the greatest inhibitors of our own success. The limitations we create for ourselves can compel us to avoid a journey towards greatness entirely. This manner of thinking can prevent growth and create a stagnant mindset. Instead of limiting our mindsets with fears, the prospect of failure should be embraced as part of the process in obtaining success. We can choose faith over fear!

Mountain climber, Craig DeMartino's mind-blowing experience is a perfect example of embracing failure as part of success. During a climb with his wife at Sundance Buttress in Rocky Mountain National Park, he fell 100 feet to the ground. A tree broke his fall on the way down and prevented him from losing his life. DeMartino sustained several life-threatening injuries including a broken neck and a fractured spine. One would think this horrible accident would have put him into early retirement. Instead, Craig chose to have his right leg amputated so that he could get a prosthetic and continue to climb. His resilience and willingness to accept the downs that come with the ups were well rewarded. He made history by becoming the first amputee to climb the Nose on Yosemite's El Capitan in less than a day. He also won the Adaptive Climbing National champion twice and placed third at the Adaptive World Championships…twice!

In a 2015 interview with Climbing.com, Craig closed the article with a powerful message that speaks to the importance of accepting failure as a positive. He said, "I've had multiple people ask me, 'If you could back up and change everything, would you go back and not have the accident?'" he continues. "And it sounds really stupid, but I wouldn't change it now. The better of the two climbers is the climber today."

Craig's true journey began that fateful day when he fell from the anchor of that range. His conscious decision to overcome all physical injuries and potential mental blocks was a matter of reclaiming his life or falling into despair. Craig was able to make this decision because he adopted a limitless mindset; free of fear and open to possibilities.

Whether it's a personal or professional challenge, we all have our metaphorical mountains to climb. We each have that one, glorious peak deeply set into the deep recesses of our minds that begs us to plant our respective flags of achievement. That peak, boldly disrupting the landscape of the sky, represents a goal we must accomplish to fulfill a greater sense of purpose for our lives. The journey upward is frightening because great heights imply long, hard falls. The fall is the lesson. The lesson creates strength and confidence to continue to move forward towards your dreams.

The reason falling, or failing, can intimidate success is because the self-doubts make us believe that we can't overcome setbacks. This limiting perspective must be shifted by changing your mindset. We must believe that failure is a stepping-stone toward success.

According to the National Science Foundation, a whopping 80% of our everyday thoughts are negative. Eighty percent! That means, during any given day, a person spends the majority of their time focused on limiting, self-limiting ideas rather than uplifting themselves with positive inner dialogue. Hollywood actor, Chris Pine once said, "The only thing you sometimes have control over is perspective. You don't have control over your situation. But you have a choice about how you view it." The key to mastering one's destiny is the ability to shift perspective; thus, controlling the outlook on any given situation. We can learn to flip the natural negative script and think at a higher level, thus a peak performance mindset.

Growth Mindset Vs. Fixed Mindset

Dr. Carol Dweck, one of the pioneers in the field of the Mindset says, "The only thing that separates people who succeed from those who don't is whether or not they have a growth mindset." You don't want to get stuck in a rigid and repetitive mindset that keeps inhibiting your potential for success.

People with a fixed mindset have a tendency to stay locked with self-imposed limitations and negative ideas. Remaining mentally rigid, people with a fixed mindset see life with inelastic boundaries; resulting in a rigid belief that they can not overcome their circumstances.

Example of a Fixed Mindset:

"I didn't make my quota this month. I'm a failure. I should quit my job."

On the other hand, individuals with a growth mindset will break through challenges and push past boundaries to find solutions to problems. People with this mindset practically apply solutions and don't give up; regardless of how rigorous a challenge might be. They are more successful because they see adverse circumstances as stepping stones instead of a brick wall.

Example of a Growth Mindset:

"I didn't make my quota this month. I will ask my team leader for performance feedback so that I can work on areas that need improvement."

Adopting a growth mindset is the key to removing inhibitions that can block us from obtaining success. Shifting toward growth requires that we embrace the adventure of stepping outside of our comfort zones. I'll never forget one moment in particular when I experienced the discomfort that comes with growth. When I was in high school, I had to do a talk about Optimism in front of 500 people. Before I started my talk, my Mom asked if I had butterflies. I said, "yes." She said, "well, that's a good thing." My Mom taught me that in life nervous or slightly uncomfortable feelings in challenging situations were positive emotions because it meant that I was growing. Her words propelled me forward towards developing a growth mindset.

Everyone has their own unique mountain that represents their personal goal or challenge that will require us to step outside of our comfort zones and take this journey to the top. The mountain can be a personal goal like physical fitness or purchasing one's first home. Some of us have a professional peak to reach. Perhaps that mountain represents hitting sales goals and increasing revenue or making a vertical shift from sales representative to a leadership role and beyond.

Whatever that mountain represents, it has finally manifested before your feet. What was once a dream has become a reality; enrapturing all of your senses. You can see it with earnest, awe-struck eyes. You can touch it with trembling fingertips. You can hear the sound of the wind rushing towards the apex. You can smell an invigorating freshness in the air that you've never inhaled before. Most importantly, you can taste the sweet nectar of success dripping on the tip of your tongue and you want more. The time to ascend has begun.

Chapter 2:
Live On Purpose with a Purpose

Your initial decision to realize a dream has led you to the base of this mountain. There it rests, high at the top, gleaming brightly like a beacon casting a brilliant light towards the sky. All of those moments enraptured within the beautiful passions illustrated across your mind are closer to becoming the waking life you've wanted for so long. As you build your mindset to reach peak performance while taking this journey, reaching the goals set in place will become easier to achieve every step of the way.

Every Success Story Starts With a Dream

What is a dream? Dreams are functions of the imagination. They are a projection of your spirit's passions and offer a glimpse into an ideal way of living. Whether these dreams reveal themselves while you sleep or if you find yourself daydreaming about new ideas that can improve your life, these dreams should not be ignored. A dream can be the seed that grows into a tree that is larger than life.

In a 2012 study conducted by Harvard psychologists, they found that people spend 47% of their time; awake, daydreaming. Spending almost half of our waking consciousness with our minds elsewhere might seem to be an inherent function of human laziness. In actuality, neurologists have discovered that when daydreams occur when we are bored or dissatisfied, the human mind begins to counter the present reality with new ideas to improve the situation at hand. Recall your childhood. Do you remember moments when you'd find yourself gazing out of the window in a classroom; imagining someplace else you'd rather be? That was your mind's way of coming up with solutions to change your present state of existence. So, the next time you find yourself fantasizing about a new idea to help boost your career, take it more seriously than a simple flight of fancy. That dream can be the conception of an action that can change the world.

Jeff Bezos, CEO and founder of Amazon.com, is a living example of a dream's potential. Before he started Amazon, he was quite successful in his position as a senior vice president at Wall Street investment firm D.E. Shaw & Co. At only 30 years old, he was the youngest senior VP in the firm's history and earned a generous six-figure salary. However, no one knew that Bezos' interests and passions did not exist in this buttoned-down world of finance.

In 1994, the world of internet retailing was in its infancy. Jeff saw the potential and dreamed of creating his own imprint in within the digital world. He took a tremendous risk and embarked on his journey to make that dream into a reality by starting an online bookstore named Amazon and was ultimately met with great reward. In less than five years after its inception, Amazon.com became the global blueprint for e-commerce operations. Over time, Bezos expanded his business by adding other products to the website. As the website's offerings continued to grow, so did revenue. With over 310 million customers, Amazon's net earnings cleared a whopping $756 billion dollars as of 2019. Bezos transformed his dream into a multi-billion dollar reality and ultimately shaped the landscape of consumerism in both digital and brick and mortar spaces.

Like Bezos, we all have the potential to turn a dream into a reality and specific steps must be taken to get there. This is where the first challenge towards manifesting an impassioned idea begins. A plan must be set in place if a dream is to be realized. If not, these designs of a charmed life will continue to exist solely in the mind. The action of extracting dreams into reality begins with the implementation of setting goals.

Go For The Goal

Edwin Locke, psychologist and founder of the Locke Goal Setting theory once wrote, "Every person's life depends on the process of choosing goals to pursue; if you remain passive you are not going to thrive as a human being." A goal is the mental process of turning a dream into an objective. It is the first step towards taking an abstract concept that exists solely in the mind and making it real. A goal, however, is about as useful as a dream if a plan of action is not set in place.

When I was a teenager, my Mom made it a point to instill a goal-oriented attitude within me. Every year, we sat down together to discuss dreams that I had and goals I wished to pursue. They could be simple goals like raising my biology grade or perhaps saving enough allowance to purchase a cool pair of boots I saw at the mall. As I grew in this process, we eventually set goals for key areas of importance in my life such as spiritual, fitness, financial, career, community impact, family, and personal development goals. She taught me to write my goals down and we would revisit the list every month and quarter to discuss my progress. In this process, my Mom taught me how to visualize my goals, create plans to achieve them, and be accountable for following through with my plans. My Mom's lessons stuck with me all throughout my life, guided me throughout my journey towards success. Today, I instill the same goal-setting technique within my own children and impart my knowledge to all who choose to reach a peak performance mindset.

The Bigger The Why, The Bigger The Try

As your brain becomes more conditioned to adopt a goal-oriented mindset, you'll begin to see meaningful, life-affirming goals take shape from the initial dreams you started with. Becoming a successful executive and entrepreneur defined my ambition at the time, but it didn't necessarily define me. Over time, I came to the realization that my choice to continue my journey to the top and beyond has to be greater than who I am as an individual. After lots of why's and tries, I clearly saw that the meaning behind everything I choose to do is for the upliftment, security, and profound love that I have for my children. They are greater than myself and they have given my goals and life great purpose. They are truly the "Why" behind many of my "What's'"!

In my own life, I've had to ask myself a series of "why's to gain an understanding of the purpose that drives me to run a successful firm and live a peak performance lifestyle. For example, I am a fitness enthusiast. While my initial motivation to live healthy was rooted in my own personal desire to be fit, asking myself the "why's" lead me to greater purpose behind my goal; compelling my ambition to work towards something greater than my own vanity. Why is fitness important to me?

Yes, I wanted to prolong my life, but again...why? Why do I want to live longer? The answer was clear as day. I wanted to live a longer life so that I can watch my children's children grow up and celebrate life with them!

When I figured out the big "why, I was more equipped to plan towards reaching my goal and found the stamina to take the journey because the purpose of my goal was greater than myself. The next step in planning my goals was to answer the "what". In this case, I had to figure out what I would do to level up in my overall goal for optimal fitness. So, I decided to run the Chicago marathon. Reaching the finish line of a race that attracts over 45,0000 participants looks great on paper. The reality? My body was not prepared to endure 26.2 miles of urban terrain and lead me to ask the third question. "How?"

How was I going to mentally and physically prepare myself for this huge marathon? After some deliberation, I decided to commit to a workout schedule where I ran three times a week for 30-45 minutes, one long distance run once a week, and a weekly yoga class. Needless to say, I completed the marathon and the moment I crossed that finish line, I knew that I hit a milestone on my journey towards becoming healthier for my family. In setting goals, it is important that we clearly know our Why behind the goal, the What, which is the goal itself, and then we create specific, measurable, and time-oriented steps to reach the goal - the Hows. I believe the bigger the why, the bigger the try and the better the how!

Get An Accountability Partner

Whether it is your employer, your colleague, or a loved one, you need someone that is vested in your growth to share your goals and dreams with. An accountability partner can provide honest feedback on your progress and offers encouragement to help reach your goal. Honest feedback can provide you with the information on how to improve your directive. Together, your plan can be analyzed what you're doing right and modify actions that aren't working.

Commit Yourself To It

Are you committed to your goal? Commitment to a goal can be measured by how much an individual is attached to a goal and how far they're willing to go to achieve it. Those with a strong commitment exhibit more endurance during challenging obstacles in the way of accomplishing goals and are more likely to reach them. Those with less commitment are more likely to give up when times are tough. When you set your goals, you must make a conscious commitment to them in the long run if you expect to achieve.

Again, this is why an accountability partner is essential when setting goals. While you may have the will of Samson to achieve, an accountability partner serves as a respected force you have to answer to; thus, fortifying your commitment to the goal. When the quarter neared to a close and the date to review my progress with my mother approached, I was excited to share the milestones I'd accomplished with someone I loved and respected. Conversely, if my progress was poor, I didn't look forward to progress meetings because I didn't want to disappoint her. Even in those moments when I didn't do my best, it encouraged me to do better and commit more to my goals and plans.

Be Clear

Are your goals clearly outlined? If a goal is too vague, creating a plan of action will be more difficult because the intentions are not clear. When my mother showed me how to discuss and write my goals down, I was able to see what I wanted to achieve clearly. Creating a plan to reach my goal became easier to navigate. A concise goal laid out visually offers understanding of the work involved on the road ahead. One mistake a lot of us make is writing our goals down and never looking at them. If we have clear steps to achieve our goals, we need to put those into action on our calendars so we can truly make our goals reality. Make it a point to review your goals monthly and write your "How's" in your schedule.

Did you know that 92% of people that set New Year's goals never achieve them? Research shows that when people put their goals in writing, they have a far greater chance of reaching success. Goal setting begins with the first question "what" do you want for yourself? Second, why do you want it? Remember, the bigger the why, the bigger the try and the better the how. We also need to be clear about the obstacles and also develop a winning strategy for navigating around the obstacles. So, write down those goals, but not just once! Rewrite and revisit those goals regularly to ensure that action is being taken towards your journey to the top!

Make Deadlines

If you've ever worked at a job, I'm certain you have experienced the concept of a deadline. Well, the same concept is required when it comes to setting goals for yourself. As you lay out your plan, give yourself a set date to accomplish each step towards your goal. Be sure to share your deadlines with your accountability partner so that he or she can make sure you remain committed to meeting them. As each date passes, with a milestone achievement in tow, you'll be a step closer towards reaching your goals.

Challenge Yourself Within Reason

If you decide to purchase your new dream car a month from now, but your finances and credit are in shambles, how likely will you be able to achieve this goal? We all have certain limitations as we begin our journey toward reaching goals. In the beginning, make sure that you have the resources necessary to hit the mark. Do you have time constraints? Do you anticipate limited funding setting you back? While it's admirable to set your goals high, you still must be realistic and reasonable. If you overshoot your ability to reach a goal, you can easily become discouraged if it doesn't happen. Keep in mind, it is still possible to reach your goal, but if circumstances seem impossible, it's time to ask yourself that big why?

Perhaps owning the new car is a component of a greater purpose like a complete lifestyle change. So, instead of spinning your wheels trying to figure out how to buy a new car in 30 days while your bank account gives you a mean side-eye, figure out how to place yourself in a better financial position so that buying your new dream car will be as easy as buying a gallon of milk.

The journey towards reaching the peak of that mountain top is a long-term expedition. When you take that first step towards this life-changing endeavor, you must be prepared for the journey ahead. You must make the decision to commit to reaching the top regardless of the risks and obstacles that you might face along your climb up this mountain. The prospect of getting to the top can be exciting and you might be compelled to run towards it. Before you lace up your shoes and start sprinting, keep in mind that impulsivity and lack of planning can wear you out before you get halfway there. Pace yourself. Make a plan and stick to it. Grab an accountability partner to keep you on track. Set time limits to ensure your progress. Above all, always ask the big "why's" so that your journey to excellence leads you to a higher purpose.

Chapter 3:
Nothing To Fear

This majestic wonder, this dream that needs to be realized, massively towers overhead. It's only natural to feel waves of intimidation coursing throughout the body. Your greatest accomplishment in life is right there, ready to be claimed. All you have to do is believe in yourself enough to step outside of that horizontal, comfort zone and make that climb upwards. So, what's the hold up? Don't just stand there, gape-mouthed, staring towards the sky. Go for it!

For some, jumping into a new endeavor comes easily. For most, it takes pre-emptive mental reprogramming to prepare for intense challenges. As the creators of your own negative thoughts, you are the only true obstacle that stands in the way of your own success. Studies have shown that 80% of success is breaking through mental barriers and serves as further evidence that the power to change the trajectory of your life primarily comes from within.

I recall an occasion that my son went on a family ski trip. As he looked at that steep decline, realizing that this was the highest elevation he'd ever experienced in his young life, he became frozen with fear. "I'm afraid, mom," he whispered through trembling lips. His fear was so intense that he tried to convince himself that he could not do it. Over and over again, he repeated to himself, "I can't do it." As he stood there, letting fear overwhelm him, he compared himself to his younger sister who seemed to have no issue skiing down this mountain at all.

"She's better than me."

"She's faster than me."

"She's braver than me."

This simple string of self-defeating words ran the risk of becoming engrained within his mindset. The fear was taking hold of his mind and creating limitations for my son in that moment. I shifted his horrified gaze from the slope and made sure I connected deeply with his brilliant, blue eyes.

I firmly told him, "What you believe will be. You WILL do this and if you believe that you CAN."

I then pointed out the only difference between him and his sister was in their mindsets. She wasn't a more skilled, more adept skier. As a matter of fact, he was the more experienced skier of the two. Her distinction rested squarely on bravery. His sister did not let fear hold her back from making that run. The message resonated with my son. He made the choice to shift his manner of thinking and sets his sights towards his goal instead of cowering from an opportunity to succeed. Needless to say, he conquered the mountain and his fear. By the end of the day, he ripped that slope several times all by himself!

My son's decision to turn his fear into courage was a transformation that anyone is capable of doing and we'll explore that shortly. Right now, let's take a look at his little sister. She was only 7 at the time and was a prime example of a certain fearlessness that most of us possess as young children. She decided that she wanted to shred that slope and she went for it, with no fear in her heart.

Fearlessness and ambition can literally be a simple, enviable jaunt from point A to point B for these little people. What if adults could capture that raw focus, determination, and fearlessness many children so effortlessly possess? How do adults grow from optimistic fearlessness into pessimistic fearfulness? At some point in life, we decide to agree with the doubts that come from fears; subsequently limiting our possibilities by creating inelastic, unnecessary barriers and negative outcomes.

The Implanted Mindset

Most negative thought patterns stem from subconscious childhood memories. Dr. Seth J. Gillihan penned an eye-opening article for Psychology Today regarding the effects of childhood experiences on adult psyches. He wrote, "Children buy into all the things they are told about themselves. If those things are negative—that they are worthless, lazy, stupid, ugly, a failure, or will never measure up to a sibling—it can leave them feeling both unworthy of a better life and powerless to change." Whether it was a handful of fear inducing experiences or an entire childhood rooted in trauma, those memories and associated feelings leave an indelible mark on the subconscious. This phenomenon is part of the implanted mindset.

The implanted mindset contains more than the negative experiences people endured as children. There are moments throughout life that leave positive impressions as well. Perhaps there was a moment when you looked over and saw your parents proudly cheering for you at a game. Maybe you had a care-taker that encouraged your budding passion for science. When we recollect our past experiences, we can use the implanted mindset to support our positive thinking habits. Instead of remaining stuck in harsh criticism from a caregiver 30 years ago, remind yourself of the edifying care takers, family members and friends that offered encouragement.

Like I always say, we can think of our mindset like a garden, you have to water the flowers, pull the weeds, and throw out the rocks. Most of us have a rock or two - a big heavy childhood experience that we can choose to throw out of our garden, so it doesn't negatively impact the rest of our lives. We can look back on sweet memories and continue to water those flowers, and the not so great things that may have come from our parents or caretakers - throw out those weeds! We are not victims of our past - we get to choose!

The majority of people choose to water the weeds instead. As we mature into adulthood, we learn the dangers of careening down icy slopes at high speeds. We hear stories about adventuresome daredevils meeting unfortunate fates when they attempted the seemingly impossible. These cautionary tales create fear that becomes deprecative, doubtful thoughts implanted within the mind.

So, when an amateur skier finds himself at the top of a very steep slope, clenching nervously to his poles, he might decide to give up and avoid the risk altogether. Instead of submitting to fear and missing out on the exhilaration that comes with championship, a better solution is to overcome that mental obstacle known as self-doubt. That fear-based mindset must be assessed, refuted, and replaced with a new imprint for success.

The Imprinted Mindset

General, military strategist and philosopher, Sun Tzu once wrote in his book Art of War, "If you know your enemies and know yourself, you will not be imperiled in a hundred battles. He then added, "If you do not know your enemies nor yourself, you will be imperiled in every single battle." Sun Tzu's words can directly apply to the inner battle between the inner critic and the dreamer. Having a clear, strong sense of self and identifying one's enemies is tantamount to succeeding at any given goal. In this case, negative thoughts are the enemy. They must be identified, neutralized, and replaced with a positive outlook.

Our imprinted mindset is developed by things and people we let speak into our lives to help us develop into who we are fully created to be such as coaches, mentors, motivational speakers, books we choose to read. We can assess where we need some development and choose a mentor who is successful in that area or read a book to learn more about that. These connections we purposefully create develop our imprinted mindset.

Let Mentors And New Heroes Imprint Your Mindset

Everyone needs edification when the decision is made to adopt a peak performance mindset. One way to get that needed support is by reaching out to someone who has taken the journey you've chosen and has succeeded. Adopting a mentor is an excellent means of creating a personal experience that ultimately builds your imprinted mind. A mentor can help you discover hidden abilities while helping to develop new behaviors for success. He or she can help you remove limiting self-beliefs while teaching new beliefs systems that can greatly impact your trajectory towards excellence. Most importantly, a good mentor will hold you accountable and keep your feet to the fire; compelling you to remain focused on your goals.

Mentors are wonderful to help refine your imprinted mindset on a personal level. We can also look outside of accessible individuals and find new heroes with notable achievements. Think of the challenges you have at hand and find someone with a similar challenge that managed to overcome it. Read their books, listen to their podcasts, and follow their social media accounts. Study what they've done to remain positive and ambitious despite seemingly insurmountable challenges and learn the steps they took to get past it.

The Inspired Mindset

When negative thoughts are released, the mind becomes open to inspiration. You have abandoned fear and inspiration has taken its place. Now, it's time to reinforce and empower that positive, constructive mindset. Sustaining positive, productive thinking habits is done by keeping an inspired mindset. Billionaire entrepreneur, Richard Branson once said, "My professional inspiration has no separation from my personal inspiration: it is people who will stop at nothing to make a positive difference to other people's lives." He admits that he can attribute his success to finding inspiration in accomplished individuals that he admires.

I knew of two top ranking sales representatives for a relatively large advertising company in Chicago. Carla and Denise started working for the company at the same time and I met them after they had been there for 2 years. Carla was at an advantage because her previous employer was the company's competitor. During her time at the other job, she built a substantial client base which she brought over to her present company.

Carla was an ideal hire because she knew the ropes, walked the talk, and arrived with new business in tow. Denise, on the other hand, had very little experience in sales and absolutely no background in supply distribution at all. What got her hired was her ambition to succeed and willingness to learn.

Within the first month of hiring, Carla ranked first in sales. Her achievement was pretty effortless considering that most of her numbers came from signing up old clients as new business for the firm. Instead of feeling threatened, Denise became inspired by Carla. She knew that at some point in her career, Carla started out much like her and she wanted to get on Carla's level. Fortunately, for Denise, Carla was more than happy to share her knowledge about the industry.

Denise asked questions, observed, and went out on sales calls with her champion colleague. In learning, Denise became aware of her hindrances and strengths and worked to refine them. She quickly learned that her sales approach was softer than Carla's and worked on fine tuning her natural ability to achieve the close rates she wanted. With each victory won, Denise found inspiration within by reflecting on the success as a result of her dedication. By the end of that year, Carla and Denise became the company's top sellers.

Denise's experience is a prime example of taking inspiration from others and using it to help you grow in a way that's best for you. She realized that she wasn't as aggressive and gregarious as Carla, so she didn't try to mimic her. She stayed authentic to herself and was able to utilize her own, unique personality to succeed. In the end, Carla and Denise's shared blueprint earned proverbial houses for both women at this company, but those houses were built by completely different means. The house of your dreams is much like the mountain that stands wide and high in front of you. All of the tools necessary to stake claim at the top can be found right within your being.

Inspiration from outside sources is a fantastic means of empowering the mind to push inhibiting limitations. However, the most powerful source of inspiration exists within. There is a flickering spark deep inside of your spirit that beckons to grow into an unfettered flame. Tucked within its center are the passions that fuel your purpose for living. This spark requires kindling to glow brightly. Media mogul Oprah Winfrey once said, "Work on the alignment of your personality and the gifts you have to give with the real reason why you are here." Like Carla the sales rep, she had the ability to be wholly aware of her capabilities as an individual. She focused on the attributes, strengths, and talents within that made her unique. Carla successfully cultivated her inner magic to hit the heights of professional achievements on her own terms.

I was fortunate to have a living blueprint for success right in my childhood home. Mom taught me to embrace life and live with intention. She was truly my inspiration and has made the greatest impact on my life. She was a stunning woman who soared as both an executive and a parent because of her optimistic perspective on life. Even when she suffered through cancer, she did so with grace and still lived life to the fullest. I so admired her ability to push through any physical or emotional pain she experienced. Her ambition to experience all the possibilities life had to offer was remarkable. Despite the unflinching gaze of mortality that mercilessly stared her down towards the end of her life, she bravely looked beyond the reality of her condition determined to savor all the beauty of life's offerings. To this day, I still hold on to her living lessons of resolve, strength, and strong will whenever I find myself confronted with my own difficult mountain to climb.

Inspiration from Within

Celebrities, colleagues, and companions are great resources to find inspiration. However, the most illuminating inspiration comes from within. You are your own hero and your inspired mindset is essentially your inner magic. It is the mark you want to make on the world.

Bruce Lee, Hollywood and martial arts icon, once said, "Always be yourself and have faith in yourself. Do not go out and look for a successful personality and try to duplicate it." He's not wrong. We can find inspiration from other sources outside of ourselves, but at the end of the day, how successful can someone be if they aren't honest with themselves and living authentically? By following another person's blueprint right down to the smallest square inch, a copy is created. If everyone simply copied each other, the world would be full of clones. How dull! One truly achieves success by improving their individual being and not by pretending to be someone else.

Tapping Into Your Inner Magic

Take a few moments to reflect on what you want out of life and ask yourself, what is the mark that you want to make in your life? Envision the mark you'd like to make. Can you see it clearly? How does it feel to be in that position of purpose? As you reflect on and visualize your goal, your inner magic begins to grow, and you feel inspiration flowing from within. Now, think of who you are as a person. What is your personality type? What talents do you have that can help you along your journey? Be sure to speak about your purpose to a trusted partner who supports your desire to grow. There is magic in speaking the spirit's intent outward from within. Like the elders say, "speak it into existence and it shall be."

When surrounded with the power of inspiration and fully tapped into inner magic, the naysayer tucked deep within the subconscious will be silenced. The volume of "I can't" has faded into silence and replaced with a thunderous, "I can". With that bright fire of inner magic burning within and a refreshing sip from a deep, cool well of inspiration, you are ready to take on that mountain and elevate to the extraordinary heights of a limitless mindset.

Chapter 4:
Optimism Always Wins

Former British Prime Minister Winston Churchill once said, "A pessimist sees the difficulty in every opportunity; an optimist sees the opportunity in every difficulty." There is so much profound truth in the simplicity of that quote. Every mountain faced can either be perceived as a painstaking deterrent or a moment to shine. The difference depends on how the person standing before that mountain chooses to approach it.

Optimism vs. Pessimism

There is no shortage of people in the world who choose to walk through life with a perpetual thundercloud overhead. These negative nellies don't stand a chance when it comes to succeeding within any capacity because they will not permit themselves to accept the possibility of life working in their own favor. Sometimes, they project their toxic thought patterns onto those around them; spreading gloom and bringing morale down. They might find temporary relief in moments of expressing negative emotions, but this is not a healthy mindset for anyone with a strong desire to lead and succeed.

Neuroscientists observed that optimistic people with positive attitudes generally have stark differences in life experiences from people with negative attitudes. In clinical findings, doctors have found that optimists find permanence in good experiences and see bad events as transient moments. Maintaining a positive disposition results in:

- Leading happy, fulfilling lives

- Developing edifying relationships
- Living longer, healthier lives than their pessimistic counterparts

Pessimistic people, on the other hand, have the exact opposite perspective from optimists. Pessimists view positive experiences as out of the ordinary, impermanent events. Bad experiences confirm their beliefs that negative conditions are the norm. Pessimism can result in:

- Higher incidences of depression and anxiety
- Poor work performance
- Unsatisfying, disconnected interpersonal relationships
- Shortened life-expectancy

Pessimists instinctively look down at the worse-case scenario when confronted with a task at hand. They don't take the time to look for the character-building nuances in front of them; nor do they crane their necks upwards to see the heights they can soar.

How can anyone climb a mountain if they refuse to look up?

The differences between optimists and pessimists are easy to observe. Within professional environment, these two personality types have completely different productivity outputs, levels of morale, and overall performance capabilities. Optimists generally outperform negative peers. Statistics have proven that within sales, optimistic sales representatives sell at 21% higher than pessimists the first year and a whopping 57% by the second year.

Psychotherapist Amy Morin wrote about the impact of negative thinking in an article for Psychology Today. She states, "A pessimistic, dismal outlook can take a toll on your life in more ways than you might think." She goes on to say, "Research consistently links **negative thinking** to an increased risk of mental health problems, physical health issues, relationship problems, and financial trouble." Making the choice to remove unhealthy thought patterns from the mind can really be a matter of life and death.

Optimistic people flourish in the workplace, but that's not where the benefits end. Adopting a positive mindset has been clinically proven to support physical wellness as well. According to the Mayo Clinic, a positive attitude can:

- Lower levels of distress
- Strengthen resistance to the common cold
- Improve psychological and physical well-being
- Improve cardiovascular health and reduced risk of death from cardiovascular disease
- Improve coping skills during hardships and times of stress

Maintaining a positive attitude requires a combination of mental and physical lifestyle changes. Surrounding oneself with encouraging people, exercising, and verbalizing self-affirmations are excellent ways to stay on a brighter, productive and positive path. Studies have also shown that transforming your perspective to accept positivity can and will directly improve professional performance. Let's take a look at some additional benefits that occur through adopting a happy mindset.

Renewed Energy

When feeling sluggish and tired, most people reach for a cup of coffee or other caffeinated beverages. While that burst of energy from the bitter buzz of a cup of black coffee can widen tired eyes in a flash, the inevitable caffeine crash will occur before the day is over. Studies have shown that a positive mindset boosts mental and physical energy levels by 23%! So, instead of reaching for that third latte to keep that momentum going, try making a concentrated effort to shift perspective in a positive direction.

Peak Productivity and Success

Once the brain is trained to brew its own serotonin-rich blend of energizing goodness, the resulting increase in stamina concurrently raises productivity output by 31% and success achievement by 38%.

Creativity Abound

As stated earlier, negative thoughts pollute 80% of daily thoughts. Those thoughts undoubtedly limit the freedom to dream and create because that pessimistic inner-critic is pretty quick to shoot down unconventional ideas. When we release negative thinking and commit to happy mindsets, that inner-critic is muted and the freedom to be creative becomes limitless.

Crushing the Rose-Colored Glasses Myth

Have you ever heard someone use the expression, "rose-colored glasses"? When people use this phrase, often within the context of a romantic relationship, they equate wearing such eyewear as a negative aspect in another person's character; pointing to naivete. It's time to reevaluate this idea. Perhaps that rosy perspective is exactly what's needed to reinforce a positive mindset.

For instance, a gentleman named Tom has a new girlfriend. The people in his life are familiar with Tom's past romantic relationships and are skeptical about his ability to make good choices when it comes to women. However, Tom, the eternal romantic, refuses to give up on finding his true love. His friends and family tell him, "Hey, Tom! Take off those rose-colored glasses, man! Do you want to get your heart broken again?" Tom had a few disappointments in the romance department. Some might even go as far as to call his love life a downright train wreck. What the naysayers don't see is that Tom has learned from his past failures in relationships and has grown emotionally and intellectually. If Tom takes off his glasses and opens his mind to the external opinions of others, he might start to view this woman from a vantage point of fear and miss out on the person that is the right one for him. Instead, Tom chooses to wear his rose-colored glasses and focuses on the positives. In doing this, he sets the tone for a loving relationship by operating from a place of positivity as opposed to negative conjecture.

Tom's family and friends represent the fears and negative thoughts deeply imbedded into the subconscious mind. His girlfriend represents the goal he wants to pursue. Those rose-colored glasses represent the choice Tom made to shift his perspective in a positive direction towards his targeted goal. Navigating through negativity is an impossible route to take down the path of success. By adopting a positive outlook, through metaphorical rose-colored lenses, one can prime the road for the journey towards excellence.

Rose-colored lenses are an essential accessory to wear throughout one's professional life as well and they never go out of style. Colleen, the Director of Sales and Marketing for my firm ProActivate had no experience in the industry prior to being hired. As a matter of fact, I initially hired her as my House Manager nearly 10 years ago! I immediately saw something very special in Colleen. Her optimism for life and eagerness to constantly improve herself both personally and professionally truly impressed me.

One day, in the early stages of building my company, she approached me and said, "I want to learn how to do what you do, Jamie!" I didn't even think twice about giving her a shot. After all, if I could trust her to care for my house and help with my children, I certainly could trust her to work for my company! We started slowly and she worked her way up from a part time Consultant, to full-time

Talent Manager, to the Client Success Manager and now, to the Director of Sales and Marketing, learning the ropes as she went. It was a whole new world for her, and of course she hit a few stumbles along the way. Those were the moments that I keenly observed Colleen. I needed to see how she could handle bumps in the road. As expected, she experienced the moment, rose to the occasion, learned from mistakes and optimistically remained open to improving her performance. From House Manager to the Director of Sales and Marketing, Colleen is a testimony of what positive thinking and a "can do" attitude can achieve in life.

At the risk of sounding cliché, no one ever said that life would be easy. There will always be an unexpected turn, a misstep, or an extremely devastating event that could potentially occur. When we choose to focus on mistakes and condemning ourselves to fear, opportunities for growth can slip right through our fingers. It takes great courage to see the world through rose-tinted lenses and that kind of bravery is necessary to take on that mountain.

Is it possible to be optimistic 100% of the time? It's not impossible, but realistically, life will throw curveballs that don't result in smiles and sunshine. There will be moments when the rose-tinted glasses aren't going to be immediately effective. As human beings, it is natural for us to go through experiences that trigger anger, sadness, disappointment, and other unhappy emotions. However, a positive mindset, even during life's most challenging moments, can serve as a catalyst to move forward proactively. So, when unfortunate events occur, it's okay to feel whatever negative emotions are felt in that moment. Just keep in mind that it's only a moment of misfortune and you have the power to prevent the negativity it carries from lasting an entire lifetime. We must not let our temporary circumstances preclude us from the joy and hope that is ours when we live a life without limits.

Chapter 5:
Tap Into Your Inner CEO

Professional climbers have two intersecting methods of training for climbing mountains. They must be physically fit. So, training the body is often the primary focus because climbers have to learn how to control swings using a great amount of upper body strength as a preventative measure against falls. One would imagine that is the only training an aspiring climber needs, but that's just not the case. Conditioning and strengthening the mind is just as, if not more, important as physical strength. Experienced climbers are well aware that a positive, focused mind leads the body, not the other way around. Activating our Inner CEO is the key to unleashing the true power of a peak performance mindset. All of the mental labor we've put into reprogramming a growth-oriented mindset has led up to this empowering point of this journey.

Did you know that 70-80% of our success depends on our mindset versus 20% relies on our skillset? So how can we shift our mindset to peak performance so we live fully to be all we were created to be and achieve all that we can achieve personally and professionally? Focus and discipline are the cornerstones of optimal mental conditioning. Whenever an experience, challenge, or opportunity presents itself, thoughts must be controlled in order to focus upon the task at hand. A strong resolve is required to halt regression into unhealthy thought patterns. Much like doing reps at the gym, a strong mind is built by repetitive actions to build power through resistance. Over time, the mind grows stronger and more powerful because it becomes more disciplined.

What Is A Disciplined Mind?

Every great success story starts with an individual with a cultivated, highly disciplined mind. This mindset culls champions from a sea of mediocrity.

It is the clear delineation between a seat-filler and a rising star with executive potential. A disciplined mind is the boss within; constantly challenging an individual to push intellectual boundaries and create limitless possibilities. A disciplined mind exhibits rational thinking and decision-making based on reason as opposed to emotions. It makes informed decisions by diligently acquiring information as opposed to making choices in haste. Disciplined thinkers have the ability to solve problems from a clear, unbiased vantage point. This combination of rational thought and informed decision-making create the ability to think critically, which is one of the most powerful tools for all in pursuit of leading their own lives independently or leading others.

One commonality between remarkable people in leadership positions is the disciplined mind firmly resting like a crown on their heads. They are able to withstand undesirable moments with grace and strength by adopting a permanent disciplined mindset. Steve Jobs, tech visionary behind Apple products, found himself in a volatile circumstance surrounding control of his own company. After an intense power struggle with then CEO in 1985, Steve Jobs was removed from the company he founded. An event this earth-shattering would have sent an emotionally driven person over the edge; compelling them to engage in financially draining lawsuits and smear campaigns. Interestingly enough, Jobs made the decision to focus on his thoughts and subsequent actions which were within the scope of his control.

He channeled all of his knowledge, energy, and creativity into creating a new tech company called NeXT Computer. Soon after his company began to gain traction, Jobs' ingenuity and insight led him to secure a collaboration with a new studio called Pixar, that ultimately transformed the aesthetic of Disney films and animation across the board. Over the next decade, Steve Jobs devoted his time and energy towards exploring the limitless potential of computer technology. He also humbly looked towards the mistakes he made in the past that got him removed from Apple and dedicated himself to becoming a better person and a successful leader. Meanwhile, Apple had a considerable downturn due to lack of visionary optics and ineffective, unstable leadership. In 1997, 12 years after Jobs was ousted, he built up enough personal and financial capital to acquire control of the company he once founded.

In 1985, when Jobs was stripped of everything he'd worked for, there was one thing that Apple's CEO and Board of Directors couldn't take away from him: *his mind*. Steve Jobs is a remarkable example of disciplined thinking and engaging his Inner CEO to think at a higher level in the midst of obstacles and had an incredible inspired mindset. Inspiration is a critical component of achieving limitless thinking, but without mental self- discipline to counter its emotional and unpredictable nature, very little can get accomplished. Discipline is the action needed to transform dreams into a reality.

You Are Your Own CEO

Your body is your corporation and your mind is your CEO. Mastering your mind to propel your life towards success is singularly the most critical step in transforming your mentality into a peak performance mindset.

No movement, no trajectory, no action is created unless the mind gives the body direction. A focused, constructive, disciplined mindset keeps the body active by perpetually driving an individual's ambitions. A healthy company is determined by the focused, mentally disciplined performance of its CEO. We've already discussed why a disciplined mindset is the outline of every great success story. However, what are the steps involved to mastering self-disciplined thoughts and strengthening focus?

Set A Goal, Create A Plan

Norman Vincent Peale was a 20th century American minister and author who wrote works that inspired people to think positively. He once said, "All successful people have a goal. No one can get anywhere unless he knows where he wants to go and what he wants to be or do." As stated earlier, every great success story starts with a dream and setting goals is the action needed to achieve a dream. It provides a visual focal point that can serve as either inspiration or a light in the tunnel (for moments when life gets tough). Without a plan to achieve a goal, the dream remains nothing more than a mental picture lodged within the recess of the mind.

In terms of tapping into your inner CEO, setting goals takes on a new dimension because; there is consideration of a greater whole rather than singular gratification. Remember the big why? The way a CEO operates requires the greatest why to always be called into question. When a CEO sets goals for a company, she considers every component that is part of that company. Her target for success isn't for her individual growth. She works towards building an entire entity. Accessing your inner CEO transforms your mindset into setting goals for your life in its entirety rather than focusing on singular wins. Let's say that you love to play golf and you are determined to beat your undefeated friend Gary during the next game. Your old mindset would set your goals towards victory over your arch nemesis on the green. However, with a new CEO mindset, your goal will be set towards becoming a better golfer as a whole. This mindset shift takes a passing accomplishment and turns it into a lifestyle geared towards overall growth. Isn't it better to be so great that you win every game against every competitor for as long as you live instead of being good enough to beat old Gary on the back nine?

The Mountain View

When reconditioning the mind to become more disciplined, the first step taken is a giant leap outside of oneself. Whether it's an issue at the office or a problem on the home front, keeping an unbiased perspective clears the mind for optimal focus. Now, think of a mountain. From the base of the mountain, one can only see what's in front of them and obstructions, like trees and the mountain itself can block a further line of sight. As you climb the mountain, you begin to see more features of the same environment from a higher vantage point. Once you get to the top of the mountain, you get a 360-degree bird's eye view of the entire area and beyond. From this vantage point, you can see new places that you didn't know existed in the first place; encouraging new ideas for exploring this terrain. The world doesn't necessarily seem smaller, but the view from the top allows you to see the bigger picture without the obstruction of details that once seemed larger than life.

Don't Take It Personal

When most people are closely connected to a situation, they have a tendency to respond with reactionary behavior. Emotionally charged reactions are unbecoming and counterproductive to leadership because decisions aren't made from a point of clear thinking. Situations must be viewed from an objective standpoint outside of personal emotions and bias.

In a joint study conducted by the University of Southern California and Stanford University, researchers discovered that negative emotions triggered by an unrelated past experience affects the ability to make intelligent decisions for the circumstances at hand. Another outcome is the reluctance to absorb information from any source that might inadvertently trigger ill feelings. With emotions clouding the view from that mountain top, it becomes impossible to take all matters into consideration and make good judgment.

Practice Patience

In this modern era of microwave mindsets, most westerners have a strong desire to amass as much as they can in the shortest amount of time possible. Patience, to many, is seen as weakness when the opposite is true. Exercising patience requires a great deal of inner-strength and personal resolve. Therefore, it is a key virtue in refining the mind as it becomes disciplined with an added benefit of developing emotional maturity. Chronic impulsivity is a waste of energy and time. Not to mention, bad decisions are often made under rushed conditions. In practicing patience, a person is able to gather as much information as possible to carefully consider their options and their long-term effects. There will be circumstances in life that demand immediate action from time to time, but even under the weight of that pressure, one must learn to retreat in patience and not let the situation take control of the outcome.

Your mountain is not going anywhere. The only thing that can take you away from reaching the top is your decision to turn your back to it and walk in the opposite direction. When you tap into the CEO of the company that is YOU, the ascension transforms from a possibility into a waking reality. You will become resolute and empowered by embracing this disciplined mindset. Then, before reaching the summit, you will see the mountain in its entirety with an unclouded vision as if you were hovering above its majesty. Claiming your stake is now tangible and you can see your way to the top clearly.

Chapter 6:
Breaking The Ties That Bind You

You are now climbing the mountain of your dreams with a disciplined mindset; compelling you upward with a positive outlook cheering you on within your conscious mind. As you surpass measurable feet, pitch by pitch, the earth below diminishes from your point of view. You have reached the point of no return. You have come too far to descend, and you are getting too close to your peak to give up. With every flash upward, you hit more challenging crutches that beg you to question whether or not you can make it to the top. So now what?

Self-Talk

On the surface, the phrase self-talk might seem quite similar to speaking positive affirmations to one's self. While this step in reclaiming your mind's power has shades of positive affirmations, the method is quite different. Self-talk is a rational method of teaching the mind how to reject negative thoughts through psychological techniques. Simply thinking positive thoughts isn't enough to develop a new mindset. Negative thoughts are aggressive and dangerous. They require equally aggressive, active measures to neutralize and replace them with a healthy mindset. The first step towards overriding negative self-thoughts is identifying when they occur.

Going back to my son's challenge on the ski slope my son made the choice to remove limitations from his perception by addressing negative thoughts. "I can't do this," was called into question and challenged with the proactive counter-inquiry of, "Why can't I do this?" By doing this, he actively took control of his thoughts by adopting a solution-oriented thought process.

Challenging negative self-beliefs through careful probing takes power away from fear. Essentially, that nagging critic that exists within the mind, second guessing and judging every action, must be silenced in order to move forward along a path of success. When we immediately address those negative thoughts with constructive counter-thoughts, we neutralize our minds from falling victim to a perpetually negative mindset.

"I can't do it because I'm not good enough."

"Who says I'm not good enough? I have accomplished many things before."

"What if I fail?"

"What if I succeed? Do I really want to miss out on an opportunity to achieve my goals?"

Transforming a pessimistic mindset is no easy task. Studies have shown that the average person has 60,000 negative thoughts a day making it difficult to allow positive intentions to shine through. In order to grow one's mindset, one must support positive thinking with an environment filled with people, objects, and ideas that encourage optimism.

First vs. Third

The manner in which we use our inner voice to criticize our actions can have a tremendous impact on our decisions to act. Studies show that by simply speaking to one's self in third person instead of first person, the mind is naturally inclined to challenge negative assertions.

Here is an example. Bill, a sales professional, recently got a promotion at his firm and he is stuck in a mindset of limited self-beliefs. On the first week at his new position, he made a few mistakes. He's already wrestling with anxiety about measuring up to the job's standards, so it's only natural for him to be hard on himself. Bill says to himself, "I can't do anything right."

In saying this, Bill is taking ownership of his mistake and allowing it to define him. This can be the start of a slippery slope if his opinion of himself goes unchecked. Bill should say, "*Bill*, can't do anything right." Once the verbal threat activates defense mechanisms in the brain, Bill's mind will automatically become more receptive to positive information as a means to fight negative thoughts.

The Catastrophe Scale
When things don't go as planned, some people have a tendency to catastrophize an incident that's of very little consequence in the grand scheme of things. Dropped an ice cream cone? End of the world! Lost a parking space to a wily corvette? End of Days! Repent! Whether you're late to a meeting or someone puts a red sock in a white laundry load, things are rarely as bad as they seem. It helps to put these bad experiences into perspective by comparing them to sizeable catastrophic events.

Bill's luck hasn't been the best lately. On the way to the office this morning, he got a flat tire along the interstate. With an impending meeting scheduled in 30 minutes looming over his head, Bill went into panic mode. Screaming, swearing, and kicking the tire, he turns a common mishap in life into Armageddon. Bill has to take a moment and ask himself, "is this worse than.....?" "Is a flat tire worse than filing bankruptcy?" No. "Is this worse than getting into a car accident?" No. "Is this worse than getting a diabetes diagnosis?" No.

Going through each notch of his Catastrophe Scale, Bill's flat tire faux pas becomes trivialized. He begins to think clearly and constructively; formulating a solution. He soon realizes that he wasted precious minutes fretting over the flat and changes it with the spare tire in the trunk. He might be a few minutes late for the meeting, but at least he hasn't gone broke and he still has his health.

You Are What You Say

Author Robin Sharma once said, "Words can inspire and words can destroy. Choose wisely." Considering how motivational speakers, world leaders, and celebrities of note have the power to affect the current of mass perception through what they say, it should be no surprise that words spoken to self can have the same effect as well. Ask yourself, do you want to build yourself or do you want to break yourself. If you chose the former, taking precautions with the words you choose to address yourself with will positively reinforce our self-belief systems. When approaching an event, self-talk prior to the commencement will determine the outcome of the event. The best tactic to ensure the best possible outcome is to pepper your self-talk with dialogue that speaks to success.

Self-Regulation

Nothing in life comes easy. Change is uncomfortable. Stepping out of comfort zones is frightening. Slipping into old negative thought patterns is very easy to do when we are met with unfamiliar challenges. Never forget that negativity is the dream slayer. All it takes is the acceptance of one moment of self-doubt that can begin a collapsing of everything accomplished. Negativity is the shifting rock that has the potential to destabilize a foundation and cause catastrophic landslides. There is no room for negativity in a limitless mindset.

As you grow more comfortable with adopting positive self-talk, you must build habits to ensure that your thoughts and actions align with your goals. This step is called *self-regulation*. For instance, now that Bill as learned to check his negativity at the door, the new, encouraging voice he hears compels him to follow through with a positive mindset. This is when self-regulation comes into play. Using the promotion as an example, let's take a look at self-regulation in action.

Self-Regulation in Action:
Bill decides to arrive at work two hours earlier than his scheduled time until he gets acclimated in his position. This extra time gives him the space and peace to familiarize himself with his new role before he performs supervisory duties when everyone arrives at 9:00 AM.

Through constructive reasoning, we learn to reject ownership of negative thoughts derived from mistakes and fear. In turn, those thoughts become positive affirmations that direct the path we take towards success.

Self-Activation

Most people have a preferred aesthetic for their surroundings that serves as a point of inspiration. The process of self-activation is just that; creating a personal space full of affirmative ideas. One step is to remove negative people from the environment. With all of the hard work put in to remove negative thoughts, why keep them around? They are toxic and serve no other purpose in life but to erode a person's self-worth. Once they're removed, it's time to start filling space with positive affirmations meant to define and inspire imminent success. So, what life-affirming activations can benefit a journey towards a peak performance mindset?

- Say positive affirmations out loud: ie. "Today is going to be a great day!"
- Play music that sparks joy and motivates
- Get plenty of rest to rejuvenate the mind and body
- Eat well and adopt a fitness routine

- Smile the moment you wake up in the morning
- Visualize your success
- Share your optimism with others around you
- Celebrate success

In my own life, I like to draw encouragement from my faith in by incorporating biblical scripture into my during my daily affirmations:

"I am complete in Christ" – Colossians 2:9-10

"I can do all things through Christ who strengthens me" - Philippians 4:13

"I have not been given a spirit of fear, but of power, love and sound mind" – 2 Timothy 1:7

"I refuse to worry about tomorrow, for tomorrow will worry about itself" –
Matthew 6:34

Personally, I turn to my faith to find positive affirmations. I recite these scriptures every day to keep my mindset tuned into positivity and a higher meaning:

"I am transformed by the renewing of my mind" - Romans 12:1-2

"God has a plan and purpose for my life" – Jeremiah 29:11

"I am still in Your presence, You wisely and tenderly lead me and bless me" – Psalm 73:23-24

"I believe my God will supply every need according to His riches in glory in Christ" – Philippians 4:19

"I trust God will lead me along fresh trails of adventure and watch over me" – Psalm 32:8

"I live with a spirit of gratitude and celebration!"

"I will choose presence over perfection, people pleasing or performance."

"With God, I do things afraid – with Him I step in with all my being and trust Him with the results."

There is another scripture I would like to share that speaks to the power of affirmations:

"Kind words are like honey–sweet to the soul and healthy for the body."-Proverbs 16:24

No matter what your religious denomination might be, we can all universally find the merit in being kind to ourselves. Show yourself grace by speaking positivity into your mind and spirit. You deserve to have your biggest fan cheering for you at all times....and your biggest fan is you.

Chapter 7:

Release Limitations And Climb Higher

After all of the mental reconditioning that has gotten you to these heights, the last thing you would expect is to find yourself wrestling with limited beliefs. Doubting yourself when times get tough, no matter how much has been accomplished, is completely natural. Limiting beliefs are more than doubting yourself. They are lies that you have bought into. We need to ask ourselves when we came into agreement with untruths about who we are and what we can accomplish in our lives. What are the dirty little lies you tell yourself? Who told you these lies and how do you overcome them? That moment might feel like you're back at square one again, but you're not. Who you have become during your journey has made you stronger and has prepared you for the challenges that lie ahead. It's time to take those limiting beliefs and release them; letting their oppressive weight fall to the ground while lightening your load.

Releasing Limiting Beliefs

High profile people with amazing success stories to draw inspiration from can be targeted all over the globe. However, those who can inspire us the most might be ordinary people seen every day. A hot dog vendor on a New York City street, serving his customers with a smile 7 days a week, rain or shine, can inspire dedication and tenacity to sustain and grow a business. We can find inspiration in a disabled neighbor who manages to live independently despite physical hindrances. That neighbor is a testimony of power of limitless thinking! If we're lucky, we might have a person close to us in our lives that serves as a living, breathing example of excellence.

About a decade ago, I hit a pivotal moment in my life that could have either made me or broken me. When it came to pursuing my dreams, my ambition fueled me towards making those dreams come true. Building a strong family and excelling professionally were two mountains that I was determined to surmount and climbed high to succeed. At one time, I believed I had it all; great husband, beautiful babies, and I was a rising, executive-level star at CareerBuilder. Then my dreams were crushed in an instant. Before my two children were out of diapers, a heart-breaking revelation ended my marriage. I found myself in a situation that was not part of my master plan and certainly not my dreams; a single, working mother with two small children that needed all of the love and nurturing attention that I could give. I'd always wanted a family that was whole and complete. The dissolution of my family unit made me limit my beliefs. Now, here I was faced with a future of navigating this life, this mountain, without the loving support of the person I'd chosen to take this journey with. The circumstances wounded me deeply as I wrestled with emotions like grief, anger, shame, and heartache. Out of the mixed bag of negative feelings I experienced, the most profound emotion was this deep, crippling sense of fear of the unknown. I had no idea what life was supposed to look like moving forward. I was shocked and sad, and I had a hard time trying to figure out what to do next.

So, I made a list of my losses as a result of this and decided to choose to heal, let it go, not let this experience hold me back. Then, I went to a lake and wrote each loss on a rock and then threw each rock separately into the lake one by one. Choosing to let each loss go and let go of any of the limiting beliefs associated with the loss.

At that moment, I felt that this was God's way of telling me that everything was going to be redeemed I am that rock tossed into a murky pond that refused to sink. I, too, can defy the order of things and still come out on top. Despite things not looking how I originally imagined, my family is whole. My kids, myself, and my faith ensures that my family will always be complete. I can and will continue to excel on the path I've chosen to take. I gathered the strength and will to continue my journey to the top by overcoming my losses and letting go of limiting beliefs. I choose instead of limiting beliefs to believe God redeems and restores all that has been broken! That story is now a chapter in my history, but the history book is closed.

Fast forward to several years later. Although doing well, the constant juggling act of being a single mother with a high-profile career began to challenge me at times. I was often pulled in different directions at once. Finding the balance between being a single mother of two amazing children and staying true to my professional goals of leading a successful company was a challenge. Then in an instant, my perspective shifted as I thought about how far I've come after my marriage ended. I built my own successful firm and raised two beautiful, intelligent children despite the curveball life tossed at me. I realized I had come too far to give up now. I knew that I couldn't stay where I was and descending from this point wasn't an option. Then I asked myself, "What if my peak isn't as far away as I think it is?" From that moment forward, I decided to push myself harder as I stayed on course for my journey upward.

Throughout our journey, we will face storms that threaten to take us off course. We might have doubts along the way. In my case, one of my mentors reminded me that I have a successful business and I am an incredible Mom with two amazing children. So, despite the limiting belief that I can't do both things well, I am indeed doing both things well...and so can you.

Chapter 8:
Live In The Now

Nearing the high summit, that dream which once only existed in the mind is only meters away from the taking. This was a long traveled and complex journey; testing human will and the strength of the mind. Looking down, the earth below has lost all of its features; resembling an expansive, two-dimensional mixture of greenish-brown hues. This is the point in an ascension where the only rational option is to continue upward. The point of origin is so far away that it begins to seem like a distant memory. Almost able to touch the clouds, a euphoria-inducing revelation pulsed from the brain to the heart that says, "I belong here."

There is still a considerable distance to cover before reaching the top. More challenging points along the climb will inevitably, unexpectedly appear. Along the way, mastering a peak performance mindset made it possible to face challenges. Adopting habits that reinforce a disciplined mind have become easier. Yet and still, that climb to the top can wear a person down.

The Present Is A Gift

Here is the thing about life: The past is already a done deal and the future has no guarantees. The only thing that is promised, the only thing that can be controlled, is right now. Although we might not have the ability to dictate what happens within a moment, we do have the ability to control how we receive and respond to the moment. Whether the climb is on a rock wall at the gym or Mt. Kilimanjaro, the only way to successfully reach heights is by focusing on the present moment and what's directly ahead and immediately above. Looking down, towards the ground, is a reminder of how distant comfort zones have become. Looking too high above invokes anticipation of the unknown. However, placing full attention on nuances within the moment will greatly reduce stress and anxiety about reaching the goal.

In real world context, recall the last great vacation taken. Whether it was a family trip, a couple's getaway, or a week of solitude, an entire world of joy outside of the daily grind was open for indulgence. Now, thinking back to the trip, was every moment enjoyed to the fullest or did intrusive, anxiety or somber thoughts begin to cloud the mind? While sipping that mojito at sunset on the beach, did thoughts about a week-old argument with a loved one creep in? While snorkeling and discovering vibrant aquatic life with the kids, were deadlines of unfinished projects clouding your consciousness? These thoughts of moments in the past and future outcomes yet to come can steal the joy of the moment. Nothing should get in the way of gifting the senses a full dose of a cool, oceanic breeze at the beach under a sky with an amber glow.

Nothing should ruin the memory of the looks of wonder as children come face to face with a clownfish in an underwater world. The present is a gift that is only given once and can never be returned.

Sometimes, the present isn't a seven-day holiday in the Caribbean. The present can sometimes issue obstacles. Appreciating the moment and focusing on the responsibilities at hand is an intelligent way to overcome a challenge. When stressful circumstances are present within more than one aspect of life, focus on one pressing matter at a time. For instance, when I decided to write this book, I had a difficult time figuring out the logistics of when to get it done. My schedule was already jam-packed with both family and business commitments. When would I find the time to write an entire book?

I took a deep breath and stopped myself from overthinking and focused on certainty. I was certain that I wanted to help people tap into an unlimited mindset. I was certain that I wanted to write a book that serves as a guide. My schedule was tight, but I decided to commit time each day. So, for several months, I was mindful in each moment to complete the task at hand one step at a time, not jumping ahead or back, but present every day. While I wrote, I didn't think about what had to be done later in the day or the next day. I remained in the present; focusing on each word written. The words became sentences. The sentences became paragraphs. Paragraphs turned into a page. Before I knew it, months had passed, and enough pages were created to make a complete book!

The Art of Mindfulness

A friend once shared this story with me. She said, "On a Saturday morning in lower Manhattan, my children and I walked past Roosevelt Park on the way to breakfast. We noticed a group of about

20 people following an instructor's slow and fluid movements. In unison, they brought their palms towards their chests and then pressed their palms outwards extending their hands.

My daughter pointed towards the group and asked me, 'What are they doing, mom?'

I replied, 'They are practicing Tai Chi.'

Her nose crinkled and she looked at me quizzically. 'What's tie chee?' she inquired.

'It's martial arts,' I replied. 'It's like karate but it's very slow.'

She paused for a moment and thought about my answer. Then, she asked, 'So, they are learning how to beat people up in slow motion?'

I laughed and said, 'No. This kind of martial art makes your body, mind, and soul healthy by practicing mindfulness.' That answer must have satisfied her because she was instantly less curious about Tai Chi and became more interested in our breakfast destination."

When asked to define mindfulness, I am always reminded of that Tai Chi story that my friend shared with me. The principle of this artform is to clear the mind of everything clouding it while focusing on the present through movement and breathing techniques. It is an exercise of mindfulness in its purest form. Through slow, movements, flowing like water, the Tai Chi students are not concerned about what happens after class or what happened before they showed up to the park. All that matters is the action of now; immersing all senses into the offerings of the present.

While many people might not have access to a Tai Chi class due to hectic schedules or lack of resources, the core of its purpose can serve as a guide for practicing mindfulness in a manner that works for the individual. In 2017, Forbes magazine published a helpful list of daily exercises anyone can do to develop a mindful lifestyle. The article states that everyday activities that we take for granted can be used to enhance mindfulness.

Walking

Instead of walking with a head full of random thoughts, focus on the action of walking. Pay attention to the concrete on the ground, the way your shoes feel on your feet, and the pace of your heartbeat.

Eating

Put down that phone and enjoy the meal! A lot of us have gotten into the awful habit of using mobiles devices during meals. A mindful approach to eating is to eat slowly, being aware of every bite and flavor that hits the palette. Feel the esophagus constrict when swallowing each bite.

Speaking and Listening

The art of communication has gotten lost in this era of expressing thoughts in 140 characters or less. Many people have a tendency to wait for their turn to speak instead of actually listening to what the other person is saying. In mindful communication, listening to the other person's every word and being aware of your own internal dialogue as they share their thoughts. Is clarification needed? If so, ask for it. When speaking, be thoughtful about the words chosen to relay your thoughts. Be deliberate with your language. If you need to take your time in order to curate the right words, by all means, don't rush.

Benefits of Mindfulness

Did you know that we spend 40% of our time worrying about things that will never happen? When the mind is flooded with inconsequential thoughts and unmerited worries, mental energy becomes directed away from present matters that can be controlled. An article published by The Mayo Clinic states, "Spending too much time planning, problem-solving, daydreaming, or thinking negative or random thoughts can be draining. It can also make you more likely to experience stress, anxiety and symptoms of depression." It goes on to say, "Practicing mindfulness exercises can help you direct your attention away from this kind of thinking and engage with the world around you." People who practice mindfulness experience:

- More happiness
- Have very little to no stress, depression, and/or anxiety
- More moments of calmness and peace
- Increased ability to be in tune with thoughts and emotions
- Increased openness to empathy towards others
- Improved focus

When all is said and done, adopting a mindful mentality can only serve to improve the overall quality of one's life. A sense of self-awareness becomes heightened along with awareness of other people and the present environment as a whole. As your ability to become more mindful in daily practice improves, the anxiety that comes with anticipation begins to wane. Focusing on the present, living in the now, absorbing your state of being through all of the senses is all that matters. As you climb even higher in this mindful state, you become aware of blisters on your hands and the chill on the tip of your nose. You inhale the crispness of the air at a high altitude as you continue to ascend even higher.

Before you know it, you've reached the top.

Chapter 9:
Purpose Beyond The Peak

With a light head and muscles trembling from fatigue, each step along the incline of the mountain's ridge takes you closer to the summit. Then, in a magical moment, the culmination of your dreams and hard work have led you to the place, you've fought tooth and nail to reach; in which to stand. You are here. After a climb that was essentially a mental exodus away from limitations and inhibitions, you have reached the top.

From this elevated vantage point, the majesty of this world can be seen from a coveted bird's eye view. So close that the clouds seem like they're within arm's reach, you are humbled and empowered by the limitless expanse of a brilliant blue sky. Looking down towards the earth, all of its features that once seemed larger than life have become smaller. The massive pine trees observed on the trail that lead to this mountain become a smaller part of a greater whole; transforming into deep green hues on a colorful landscape. From heights above to depths below, you are awestruck by this exquisite masterpiece of this beautiful earth.

Once your mountain has been climbed, it is important to continue to practice mindfulness and fully take in the experience of achieving that goal. Take note of your emotions. How are you feeling? Exhilarated? Intoxicated with joy? Perhaps new feelings that have never been experienced begin to surface. Take inventory of how success affects the mind, body, and spirit. Savor the moment like a well-prepared meal in a five-star restaurant. Over time, the high that comes from accomplishing endeavors will more than likely begin to dissipate as this new position in life becomes an everyday standard. When a goal is reached, one can find himself asking, "Now what?'

From Peak to Plateau

After gaining success and becoming established in this elevated plane of existence, complacency can easily replace an inspired mind. Anthony is a highly successful figure within the film industry; producing over thirty award winning films through his production company that he built from the ground up. Ever since he was a child, Anthony wanted to make movies. Both of his parents made a comfortable living in the industry. His mother was a screenwriter and his father was a film editor. They would occasionally bring him to movie sets and production studios to help inspire his budding interest in the craft.

Anthony stuck with his dream for decades; completing film school and directing independent movies that won praise from the film community. By the time he turned 31 years old, Anthony signed his first multi-million dollar directorial deal with a major motion picture studio. This was a dream come true and he was living the high life. After a few years, he became disenchanted with the Hollywood movie scene. While he appreciated the accolades, his hard work earned him, he didn't feel fulfilled. After careful deliberation, Anthony decided that he lacked inspiration and was falling out of love with visual storytelling. Finding pleasure in activities he once enjoyed became more difficult. He got tired of the same faces, the same scripts, and the same surface conversations he painfully endured in social gatherings. Despite the money overflowing in his bank account and access to power that others only dream of, he felt that he needed more out of life. He thought to himself, "what's the point of this success if it has no meaning."

Once his contract was up, he left Hollywood and moved back to the east coast in search of new stories to tell. He started his own film production company that carefully curated unique stories reflecting untold narratives throughout the globe. As his company grew, he was able to create opportunities for others. It gave him a great sense of purpose to be able to provide a platform for undiscovered talent with gifts to share with the world. Anthony took his altruism a step further and created free filmmaking programs for young people at underserved local schools. He committed his time and resources to inspire children to tell their stories the way that his parents inspired him. He continues to work with youths to this day.

    Anthony's story is a great example of what can be done to reinvigorate inspiration and ambition once there is a plateau in success. After serious introspection, he decided that his life had to serve a purpose greater than himself. The peak he reached by the time he was 31 lead him to the base of a new journey towards a new goal that he'd never considered. This was a new quest that went beyond the ego and earthly ambitions. The next mountain to climb was towards a sense of purpose and higher meaning.

Finding Purpose And Higher Meaning

Discovering purpose is an exercise in using mindfulness to draw inspiration. Once the mindset becomes inspired again, we become open to exploring options that add existential value to our lives. In pursuing a higher meaning for life, we must strive to become something bigger than ourselves and individual accomplishments. When that plateau occurs, there are methods to jumpstart a brilliant mind; making it receptive to the pursuit of a heightened level of human consciousness.

Counsel With Your Inner Child

Most passions enjoyed by adults stem from the same joys experienced as a child. Sometimes, it helps to take a quick jaunt through childhood to recall the activities and experiences that sparked interest. Did you enjoy playing school? Perhaps teaching a course might be ideal. Were you fond of building houses out of Lincoln Logs and Legos as a child? Explore that passion and see how it can help you serve the world. You can do something phenomenal with this gift from your inner child like building homes for the homeless.

Be Vulnerable

Being at the top of your game creates expectations within the people who observe you. They have come to admire the precision, discipline, and ambition you've exhibited while they watched you skyrocket towards success. When all eyes are on you, possibly studying your every move, pressure to perform under the expectations can occur. These people see you as a living example and the last thing you want to do is let them down. Such an admiration can create a hindrance when trying to move towards a path of higher meaning because these expectations can place behavioral limitations. People will expect you to behave in one manner, even if your heart wants to go against the grain of your current reality. You will have to try new approaches with spectators' gazes fixed upon your every move. The possibility of failing in front of an audience is anxiety-inducing. However, you've been down this road before. You have learned to operate outside of the limitations of fear in the pursuit of obtaining a goal. Do not be afraid to exhibit vulnerability when it comes to living your own life with higher meaning. People on the outside will always pass judgment, but your life is your own and not theirs to live.

Let New Worlds Inspire You

Breaking away from the monotony of daily life and the same social circles is a great start in finding a path towards purpose. Travel abroad to a country you've never thought to explore. Sit with the locals, enjoy their food. Learn about their customs and the problems facing their communities. Perhaps purpose lies within helping the people encountered during travels. Maybe, the new world is right in your backyard. Make connections with neighbors or civic groups in your community. Get a feel for the worlds revolving outside of your daily existence and explore new possibilities of finding your path to higher meaning.

Be Of Service To The World

At the foundation of our source of meaning, we have the ability to love, work, and play. These actions are essential for feeling good. As we advance during our quest for higher meaning, serving others and keeping our minds open to learning new things adds another layer to our purpose and joy. When we hit the peak of our purpose-filled journey, we discover the gratification of giving back to humanity and the world at large. Reaching this level of higher meaning can be one of

the greatest joys in life.

Dr. Dorothy Height famed civil rights activist once said, "Without service, we would not have a strong quality of life. It's important to the person who serves as well as the recipient. It's the way in which we ourselves grow and develop." This mindset is imperative when opening oneself up to a life of higher meaning. The lessons learned on your journey about grace, optimism, self-awareness, and self-discipline should be shared with others who will have to climb their own unique mountains one day. Impart the wisdom gained from your journey through your interactions. Encourage others to take a path towards a purposeful life in both actions and words. A limitless mindset should be infectious. Imagine how wonderful this world can be if the majority of the humans that populated it functioned from a point of mindfulness and a positive, limitless mindset. That peak, that goal, must be about greater service in the name of love. When I speak of love, it starts with those closest to you and it extends outward to serve the collective that is humanity. When we reach the top, the entire world is within our scope and therefore becomes our responsibility to ensure

Your Mindset's Peak Performance

Think back to the genesis of your journey. Recall that moment when you woke up and decided that you wanted to change your world and work towards building a greater version of yourself. That lightbulb moment sparked the steps taken to walk through the wild in pursuit of a goal that rested at the top of a mountain waiting to be claimed. Take pride in the inner battles endured as you challenged limiting belief systems implanted throughout your life in order to accept the possibility of creating new tenets under which to live. That nasty little inner critic that once arrested your will to step out of the confines of comfort zones has been silenced. With your new prescription for rose-colored glasses, you have learned to view life from a rosy, positive perspective. As the ascent grew more difficult, you called upon the strength of your disciplined mind to help you get through moments when quitting seemed like the best option. As you approached the subtle incline of the ridge, you continued to hike mindfully towards your goal at the summit. At last, you arrived at the apex and the dream that inspired your journey became a reality.

As arduous as the initial journey was, the peak represents more than the dream that inspired action to change. The goal achieved is definitely a fine compensation for tremendous effort, but the true reward is how the mind has transformed into a powerhouse of limitless thinking. At this peak, at this new beginning, anything you set your mind to is possible because you have conditioned it, reshaped it, and activated it to optimal performance. Your mind, once plagued with fear and doubts, has become a well tempered machine of precise thought and unlimited potential. Every challenge faced, every mountain that beckons to be climbed, every dream that must be formed into a reality is no longer just a possibility. Your heightened mindset makes success an inevitability.
Welcome to the TOP...

www.ingramcontent.com/pod-product-compliance
Lightning Source LLC
Chambersburg PA
CBHW021423210526
45463CB00001B/501